VPJournals
TRAVEL JOURNAL
VPJournals

Travel Journal

Costa Rica

VPJournals

ISBN-13: 978-1518844034
ISBN-10: 1518844030

Contact Details

Name:

Email address:

Tel:

Address:

Important Medical Information

Blood type:

Medication:

CONTENTS

Hi, I hope you enjoy this journal. It is packed with cool stuff and recommendations for you trip to Costa Rica, and has plenty of space to record details of your trip.

Have fun in Costa Rica!

Great Places to visit in Costa Rica

Rincon de la Vieja National Park	✓
Witch's Rock Canopy	
Puerto Uva	
Corcovado National Park	
Museo de Formas Espacios y Sonidos	
Mal País and Santa Teresa	
Jobbie's Surf Camp	
Península de Nicoya	
La Paz Waterfall Gardens	
Playa Hermosa	
Playa Tamarindo	
Monteverde	
Playa de Jacó	

Tamarindo	
Chirripo National Park	
Reventazon	
Montezuma	
Celeste River	
Las Baulas National Marine Park	
Museum of Contemporary Art and Design	
San José Costa Rica Temple	
Museo de Cultura Popular	
Add your own after researching	

Cool Places to visit in Costa Rica with Kids

Arenal Hanging Bridges	✓
Arenal Volcano National Park	
Corcovado National Park	
Corobici River	
INBio Park	
La Paz Waterfall Gardens	
Manuel Antonio National Park	
Monteverde Cloud Forest Reserve	
Parque Nacional Volcan Rincon de la Vieja	
Refugio Nacional de Fauna Silvestre Ostional	
Mal País and Santa Teresa	

Museo del Banco Central de Costa Rica	
Museo de Jade (the Jade Museum)	
Centro Nacional de Arte y Cultura (National Center of Art and Culture)	
Museo de Arte Costarricense	
Tortuguero National Park	
Parque Nacional Volcan Poas (Poas Volcano National Park)	
Parque Nacional Volcan Irazu	
Costa Rican Center of Science and Culture	
Puerto Viejo	
Add your own after researching	

Good Places to Eat in Costa Rica

Restaurant la Terrasse	✓
Park Cafe	
Taller Gastronomico El Punto	
Restaurante Grano de Oro	
Mantras Veggie Cafe and Tea House	
La Esquina de Buenos Aires	
Otoya 1155 Restaurant & Lounge	
Cafe-Te-Ria	
The Corner Pizzeria & Cafeteria	
Tin Jo	
Black Stallion Cafe & Surf Saloon	
Sprout	

Matty's DeliCafe	
La Bodega	
Cafe Tico Tamarindo	
Surf Shack Burgers & Wings	
Seasons by Shlomy	
La Princesa Cafe	
Green Papaya Taco Bar	
Lola's	
Tres Cabras Restaurante at Nepenthe	
Chifa La Familia Feliz	
Cascajo's del Arena	
Cafe Rain Forest	
Add your own after researching	

Best Websites to Research Further

Do some more research on the internet to plan your trip:

www.wikipedia.org/wiki/costarica
www.govisitcostarica.com
www.VisitCostaRica.com
www.lonelyplanet.com/costa-rica
www.CostaRica.com
www.tourism.co.cr
www.anywhereCostaRica.com
www.nomadicmatt.com/travel-guides/costa-rica-travel-tips/
www.wikitravel.org/Costa_Rica

More places I want to visit on our trip

1. ______________________________
2. ______________________________
3. ______________________________
4. ______________________________
5. ______________________________
6. ______________________________
7. ______________________________
8. ______________________________
9. ______________________________
10. ______________________________
11. ______________________________
12. ______________________________
13. ______________________________
14. ______________________________
15. ______________________________

Postcard List

Name:
Address:

Name:
Address:

Name:
Address:

Name:
Address:

Name:
Address:

Name:
Address:

Name:
Address:

Name:
Address:

Name:
Address:

Name:
Address:

Name:
Address:

Name:

Address:

Name:

Address:

Name:

Address:

Packing List

✓	This Journal
	Tickets
	Passport
	Money
	Chargers
	Batteries
	Book to read
	Camera
	Tablet
	Sun glasses
	Sun cream

	Toiletries
	Water
	Watch
	Snacks
	Umbrella
	Towel
	Guide book
	Kindle
	Jacket
	Medication
	Add more below

Costa Rica Facts

- Costa Rica has a population of approximately 4.75m and it's capital is San José

- Costa Ricans call themselves Ticos and Ticas

- There are over 130 species of fish, 220 reptiles, 1,000 butterflies (10% of the world's butterflys are in Costa Rica), 9,000 plants, 20,000 species of spiders and 34,000 species of insects

- They don't really have summers and winters, but a dry season that runs December to April and a rainy season that runs May to November

- "Pura vida" is the national saying, which means "pure life," a sunny, feel good expression used as a greeting, goodbye, or if someone asks how you are doing

- Football / soccer, is by far the most popular sport in Costa Rica

- The older generations of Ticos are not tall, so most furniture, like chairs, couches, beds, etc. are built 6-8 inches lower than in the US.

- Costa Rica is the longest-standing democracy in Central America.

- Costa Rica border Nicaragua to the north and Panama to the south.

- More than 25% of Costa Rican land is protected national parks and refuges

- The average life expectancy of 77 years is one of the highest in the world.

- The Costa Rican Colon is the currency of Costa Rica.

- They claim a 96% literacy rate. In very poor and rural areas, where children can't get to schools, they teach classes over a national radio station.

Clothes & Shoe Sizes

Children's Shoe Sizes

UK	EUROPE	US	Japan
4	20	4½ or 5	12 ½
4 ½	21	5 or 5½	13
5	21 or 22	5½ or 6	13 ½
5 ½	22	6	13½ or 14
6	23	6½ or 7	14 or 14½
6 ½	23 or 24	7 ½	14½ or 15
7	24	7½ or 8	15
7 ½	25	8 or 9	15 ½
8	25 or 26	8½ or 9	16
8 ½	26	9½	16 ½
9	27	9½ or 10	16 ½ or 17
10	28	10½ or 11	17 ½
10½ or 11	29	11½ or 12	18
11 ½	30	12½	18 or 18 ½
12	31	13	19 or 19 ½
12 ½	31	13 or 13½	19 ½ or 20
13	32	1	20
13 ½	32 ½	1 ½	20 ½
1	33	1½ or 2	21
2	34	2½ or 3	22

Children's Clothing Sizes

UK	EUROPE	US	Australia
12m	80cm	12-18m	12m
18m	80-86cm	18-24m	18m
24m	86-92cm	23-24m	2
2-3	92-98cm	2T	3
3-4	98-104cm	4T	4
3-5	104-110cm	5	5
5-6	110-116cm	6	6
6-7	116-122cm	6X-7	7
7-8	122-128cm	7 to 8	8
8-9	128-134cm	9 to 10	9
9-10	134-140cm	10	10
10-11	140-146cm	11	11
11-12	146-152cm	14	12

Women's Shoe Sizes

UK	EUROPE	US	Japan
3	35 ½	5	22 ½
3 ½	36	5 ½	23
4	37	6	23
4 ½	37 ½	6 ½	23 ½
5	38	7	24
5 ½	39	7 ½	24
6	39 ½	8	24 ½
6 ½	40	8 ½	25
7	41	9 ½	25 ½
7 ½	41 ½	10	26
8	42	10 ½	26 ½

Women's Clothes Sizes

UK	US	Japan	France / Spain	Germany	Italy	Australia
6/8	6	7-9	36	34	40	8
10	8	9-11	38	36	42	10
12	10	11-13	40	38	44	12
14	12	13-15	42	39	46	14
16	14	15-17	44	40	48	16
18	16	17-19	46	42	50	18
20	18	19-21	48	44	52	20

Men's Shoe Sizes

UK	EUROPE	US	Japan
6	38 ½	6 ½	24 ½
6 ½	39	7	25
7	40	7 ½	25 ½
7 ½	41	8	26
8	42	8 ½	27 ½
8 ½	43	9	27 ½
9	43 ½	9 ½	28
9 ½	44	10	28 ½
10	44	10 ½	28 ½
10 ½	44 ½	11	29
11	45	12	29 ½

Men's Suit / Coat / Sweater Sizes

UK / US / Aus	EU / Japan	General
32	42	Small
34	44	Small
36	46	Small
38	48	Medium
40	50	Large
42	52	Large
44	54	Extra Large
46	56	Extra Large

Men's Pants / Trouser Sizes (Waist)

UK / US	Europe
32	81 cm
34	86 cm
36	91 cm
38	97 cm
40	102 cm
42	107 cm

We have included another copy of this at the back of the book, so you can find it quickly again when you are in Costa Rica

Costa Rica Trip Diary

Write a daily diary during your trip

Day 1

Date: ______________ **Weather:** ______________

Day 2

Date: ______________ **Weather:** ______________

Day 3

Date: ____________________ **Weather:** ____________________

Day 4

Date: ______________ **Weather:** ______________

Day 5

Tip! Send your postcards

Date: ________________ **Weather:** ________________

Day 6

Date: **Weather:**

Day 7

Date: ______________ **Weather:** ______________

Day 8

Date: ____________ **Weather:** ____________

Day 9

Date: ______________ **Weather:** ______________

Day 10

Date: ____________ **Weather:** ____________

Day 11

Date: ________________ **Weather:** ________________

Day 12

Date: ____________ **Weather:** ____________

Day 13

Date: ________________ **Weather:** ________________

Day 14

Date: ________________ **Weather:** ________________

Day 15

Date: **Weather:**

Day 16

Date: ____________ **Weather:** ____________

Day 17

Date: ____________ **Weather:** ____________

Day 18

Date: ____________ **Weather:** ____________

Day 19

Date: ______________ **Weather:** ______________

Day 20

Date: ________________ **Weather:** ________________

Day 21

Date: ________________ **Weather:** ________________

Memories of your Trip

Things I will remember from the trip

Favorite Places visited on the Trip

People I Met

Name:
Address:
Tel:
email:

Name:
Address:
Tel:
email:

Name:
Address:
Tel:
email:

Name:
Address:
Tel:
email:

Name:
Address:
Tel:
email:

Name:
Address:
Tel:
email:

Name:
Address:
Tel:
email:

Name:
Address:
Tel:
email:

Name:
Address:
Tel:
email:

Name:
Address:
Tel:
email:

Name:
Address:
Tel:
email:

We hope you enjoyed your trip to Costa Rica

Please leave us a review if you found this Journal useful

Check out our useful resources on the next few pages

Clothes & Shoe Sizes

Children's Shoe Sizes

UK	EUROPE	US	Japan
4	20	4½ or 5	12 ½
4 ½	21	5 or 5½	13
5	21 or 22	5½ or 6	13 ½
5 ½	22	6	13½ or 14
6	23	6½ or 7	14 or 14½
6 ½	23 or 24	7 ½	14½ or 15
7	24	7½ or 8	15
7 ½	25	8 or 9	15 ½
8	25 or 26	8½ or 9	16
8 ½	26	9½	16 ½
9	27	9½ or 10	16 ½ or 17
10	28	10½ or 11	17 ½
10½ or 11	29	11½ or 12	18
11 ½	30	12½	18 or 18 ½
12	31	13	19 or 19 ½
12 ½	31	13 or 13½	19 ½ or 20
13	32	1	20
13 ½	32 ½	1 ½	20 ½
1	33	1½ or 2	21
2	34	2½ or 3	22

Children's Clothing Sizes

UK	EUROPE	US	Australia
12m	80cm	12-18m	12m
18m	80-86cm	18-24m	18m
24m	86-92cm	23-24m	2
2-3	92-98cm	2T	3
3-4	98-104cm	4T	4
3-5	104-110cm	5	5
5-6	110-116cm	6	6
6-7	116-122cm	6X-7	7
7-8	122-128cm	7 to 8	8
8-9	128-134cm	9 to 10	9
9-10	134-140cm	10	10
10-11	140-146cm	11	11
11-12	146-152cm	14	12

Women's Shoe Sizes

UK	EUROPE	US	Japan
3	35 ½	5	22 ½
3 ½	36	5 ½	23
4	37	6	23
4 ½	37 ½	6 ½	23 ½
5	38	7	24
5 ½	39	7 ½	24
6	39 ½	8	24 ½
6 ½	40	8 ½	25
7	41	9 ½	25 ½
7 ½	41 ½	10	26
8	42	10 ½	26 ½

Women's Clothes Sizes

UK	US	Japan	France / Spain	Germany	Italy	Australia
6/8	6	7-9	36	34	40	8
10	8	9-11	38	36	42	10
12	10	11-13	40	38	44	12
14	12	13-15	42	39	46	14
16	14	15-17	44	40	48	16
18	16	17-19	46	42	50	18
20	18	19-21	48	44	52	20

Men's Shoe Sizes

UK	EUROPE	US	Japan
6	38 ½	6 ½	24 ½
6 ½	39	7	25
7	40	7 ½	25 ½
7 ½	41	8	26
8	42	8 ½	27 ½
8 ½	43	9	27 ½
9	43 ½	9 ½	28
9 ½	44	10	28 ½
10	44	10 ½	28 ½
10 ½	44 ½	11	29
11	45	12	29 ½

Men's Suit / Coat / Sweater Sizes

UK / US / Aus	EU / Japan	General
32	42	Small
34	44	Small
36	46	Small
38	48	Medium
40	50	Large
42	52	Large
44	54	Extra Large
46	56	Extra Large

Men's Pants / Trouser Sizes (Waist)

UK / US	Europe
32	81 cm
34	86 cm
36	91 cm
38	97 cm
40	102 cm
42	107 cm

Common Translations

English	French	Spanish	Italian
Hello	Bonjour	Hola	Ciao
Goodbye	Au revoir	Adiós	Arrivederci
Yes	Oui	Sí	Si
No	Non	No	No
Please	S'il-vous-plaît	Por favor	Per favore
Thank you	Merci	Gracias	Grazie
Excuse me	Excusez-moi	Perdón	Mi scusi
How much	Combien	Cuánto	Quanto
My name is	Mon nom est	Mi nombre es	Io mi chiamo
Where is	Où est	Dónde está	Dov'è
The bank	La banque	El banco	La banca
The toilet	Les toilettes	El baño	Il bagno

German	Japanese	Mandarin	Hindi
Hallo	Kon'nichiwa	Ni hao	Namaste
Auf Wiedersehen	Sayonara	Zaijian	Alavida
Ja	Hai	Shi de	Ham
Nein	Ie	Meiyou	Nahim
Bitte	Onegaishimasu	Qing	Krpaya
Vielen Dank	Arigato	Xiexie	Dhan'yavada
Entschuldigung	Sumimasen	Duoshao	Mujhe mapha karem
Wie viel	Ikura	Wo de mingzi shi	Kitana
Mein Name ist	Watashinonamaeha	Nali	Mera nama hai
Wo ist	Doko ni aru	Yinhang	Kaham hai
Die Bank	Ginko	Yinhang	Bainka
Die Toilette	Toire	Cesuo	Saucalaya

Notes:

CPSIA information can be obtained
at www.ICGtesting.com
Printed in the USA
BVOW04s1207201117
500887BV00017B/68/P

9 781518 844034